THE SECOND WORLD WAR IN THE AIR IN PHOTOGRAPHS

1945

L. ARCHARD

AMBERLEY

First published 2015

Amberley Publishing
The Hill, Stroud
Gloucestershire, GL5 4EP

www.amberley-books.com

British Library Cataloguing in Publication Data.
A catalogue record for this book is available from the British Library.

ISBN: 978 1 4456 2255 2 (print)
ISBN: 978 1 4456 2278 1 (ebook)

Typeset in 10.5pt on 13pt Sabon.
Typesetting and Origination by Amberley Publishing.
Printed in the UK.

Contents

Introduction

1945 started with the German Ardennes offensive, the Battle of the Bulge, still ongoing on the Western Front. In the last major Luftwaffe attack of the war, German aircraft attacked Allied air bases in Belgium and the Netherlands in an attempt to gain air superiority and allow the stalled advance of the German forces fighting in the Ardennes to continue. In the Far East, USAAF B-29 bombers attacked targets in Thailand, including a railway bridge outside Bangkok. Soon afterwards they would switch to area bombing, using incendiaries to attack highly flammable Japanese cities. Later in the month, American forces in the Philippines invaded Luzon, the largest of the islands. The US naval forces off the Philippines increasingly became the target of kamikaze attacks.

February would see perhaps the most controversial attack made by the RAF's Bomber Command during the Second World War: the bombing of Dresden on the night of 13/14 February. The first force of 254 Lancaster bombers dropped 500 tons of high-explosive bombs and 375 tons of incendiary bombs on target markers dropped around a sports stadium next to Dresden's medieval old town with its congested and flammable timber buildings. When the second force arrived some three hours later, the fires could be seen from 500 miles away in the air. The second force, consisting of more than 500 Lancasters, dropped another 1,800 tons of bombs on the city. On 14 and 15 February, the city would be attacked again by the USAAF. The bombing of Dresden has been justified on the grounds that the city was an industrial centre, with factories and workers supporting the German war effort, and that it was a communications centre, the bombing of which would cause disruption that would aid the Soviet advance from the River Oder towards Berlin. Critics, however, have argued that Dresden's military and industrial importance was overrated, that it was a cultural landmark and that the bombing was indiscriminate and disproportionate to the expected military gains.

Later in the month, US Marines landed on the island of Iwo Jima, which it was hoped would be a useful strategic base for supporting attacks against the Japanese Home Islands. The island had been bombarded by USAAF aircraft and by US Navy ships and aircraft since mid-June 1944; the Japanese had plenty of opportunity to prepare their defences and so the fighting on the ground was fierce. As part of the naval task force there were several aircraft carriers, whose pilots flew close air support missions to help the Marines. General Kuribayashi, the Japanese commander on the island, was allocated only a few kamikaze pilots; the peak of the kamikaze attacks would come with the invasion of Okinawa in April.

Early in March, American troops captured the Ludendorff Bridge across the River Rhine at Remagen, the only bridge across the Rhine that had not been demolished before the arrival of Allied troops. The bridge was of such significance for both sides that US forces built up a huge concentration of anti-aircraft guns around it to protect it, while the Germans used Me 262 and Arado Ar 234 jets to try and destroy the bridge. Hitler ordered SS General Hans Kammler to fire V2 rockets at the bridge to destroy it, the only time they were fired against a German target, but the eleven rockets fired all fell on nearby towns. The V2 attacks against Britain and Belgium continued, however. March would also see the beginning in earnest of the American firebombing campaign against Japanese cities, with raids against Tokyo and Nagoya among other cities, as well as attacks on the naval bases of Kobe and Kure. This would continue in April, when another large-scale firebombing raid was carried out against Tokyo.

On 1 April Operation Iceberg, the invasion of Okinawa, began. Okinawa is only 340 miles from the Home Islands off Japan and was a potential leaping-off point for an Allied amphibious invasion of Japan. Resistance was fierce, and included the intense use of kamikaze attacks against the Allied warships off the island. The word kamikaze, literally 'divine wind', originally referred to two typhoons that dispersed Mongol invasion fleets off Japan during the thirteenth century. Kamikaze attacks were thought to be more accurate than conventional attacks and to cause more damage to the target because the fuel in the aircraft would add to the explosion; the Japanese hoped to be able to destroy large numbers of Allied ships, particularly aircraft carriers, and that this would justify the sacrifice of pilots and aircraft. On 6 April, in Operation Kikusui ('Floating Chrysanthemums'), waves of kamikaze attacks were launched against the Allied fleet off Okinawa, some 400 aircraft taking off from airfields on the southern island of Kyushu. The Japanese aircraft attacked first the destroyers on picket duty on the outskirts of the fleet, and then the carriers in the middle. Although no major Allied warships were lost (those sunk were smaller ships, especially destroyers), several carriers were severely damaged, including the USS *Bunker Hill*, which was hit by two kamikaze within thirty seconds, resulting in 389 casualties. Altogether, between 6 April and 22 June (the end of the Battle of Okinawa) more than 1,600 kamikaze took off from Kyushu, along with more from Formosa (now Taiwan; the island was under Japanese occupation from 1895 to 1945).

The British Pacific Fleet took part in the Battle of Okinawa, serving under American command as Task Force 57. The role of the British force was to neutralise the airfields in the Sakishima Islands, to the south and west of Okinawa, and prevent them from being used as bases to launch kamikaze attacks against the Allied fleet. As well as neutralising airfields, the Fleet Air Arm also played a role in maintaining a combat air patrol over the fleet as a way of protecting against kamikaze attacks, the Supermarine Seafire being particularly effective at this because of its high-altitude performance.

Meanwhile, in Europe the campaign against Nazi Germany seemed to be finally drawing towards its conclusion. Hitler was trapped in his bunker under Berlin; on 23 April, as fighting raged in the city's outskirts between the remnants of the Wehrmacht and the Red Army, Göring sent a message to the bunker, asking to be declared Hitler's successor and announcing that if he did not receive a response by 10 p.m. that day, he would assume Hitler had been incapacitated and take command. Hitler needed little persuading that this was an act of treason on Göring's part, he stripped him of his offices and his membership of the Nazi Party and had him placed under house arrest. On 9 April, a heavy RAF raid against Kiel sank the pocket battleship *Admiral Scheer*, and on 25 April Bomber Command Lancasters attacked the compound around Hitler's Alpine retreat at Berchtesgaden, the Berghof. 29 April saw the surrender of all German forces in Italy and Austria and the beginning of Operations Manna and Chowhound, a mission by the RAF and USAAF respectively to drop food supplies to civilians in areas of the Netherlands which were still under German occupation and which were experiencing famine conditions.

29 April also saw Hitler's marriage to Eva Braun in the bunker in Berlin. The following day, they both committed suicide. On 1 May, Josef Goebbels, propaganda minister and Hitler's appointed successor as chancellor, also committed suicide along with his wife. On 2 May, no longer bound by their oath of loyalty to Hitler or by Goebbels' demands, the remaining German forces in Berlin surrendered to the Red Army. German forces were now surrendering to the Allies throughout Europe and on 4 May Field Marshal Montgomery accepted the surrender of the remaining German troops in Denmark, northern Germany and the Netherlands, while Admiral Dönitz ordered the remnants of the U-boat force to cease fighting. On 7 May, Germany officially surrendered unconditionally to the Allies at General Eisenhower's supreme headquarters in Rheims. The surrender took effect from one minute past midnight on 8 May, which would become VE Day in Britain. Although a representative of the Red Army, General Susloparov, was present and signed the instrument of surrender, the Soviet government argued that he did not have the authority to do so and arranged for a second surrender to take place in Berlin, where Marshal Zhukov signed on behalf of the Soviet Union; 9 May would be designated Victory Day in the Soviet Union and remains so in Russia today. Göring, who had been released by Luftwaffe troops from his house arrest at the hands of the SS, surrendered to American troops on 7 May. On 10 May the surviving German U-boats began to surrender at Loch Eriboll, a sea loch and deep-water anchorage on the north coast of Scotland. They were escorted in groups by warships and aircraft to Kyle of Lochalsh on the west coast and then onto Londonderry Port in Northern Ireland or Cairnryan on the south-west coast of Scotland. The surrender of the U-boat force and its internment at Londonderry Port or Cairnryan continued until 30 June. On 4 June, a Short Sunderland V flying boat finished the final Coastal Command North Atlantic convoy patrol some 500 miles south-west of Ireland.

Meanwhile, in the Far East the war was continuing unabated. In mid to late May, USAAF B-29 bombers had carried out heavy raids against Nagoya and the port and naval base of Yokohama. As June began, naval aircraft from US carriers were able to carry out attacks on airbases on Kyushu in an attempt to prevent kamikaze aircraft from being able to take off and attack the fleet. On 10 July, US Navy aircraft mounted an attack on Tokyo for the first time. Later in July, US naval aircraft launched a series of attacks against Kure, attacking the Japanese naval base on 24, 25 and 28 July and sinking numerous warships, including an aircraft carrier and three battleships, at anchor there. Meanwhile, aircraft from the British Pacific Fleet attacked targets in the Inland Sea between the Japanese Home Islands and mainland Asia. However, the raids by the B-29s on the Japanese Home Islands continued; on 15 June Osaka was bombed heavily and at the end of July Kobe and Nagoya were both attacked. On 17 July, the Potsdam Conference had begun; Churchill (replaced part way through by Clement Atlee following the Labour Party's sweeping victory in the 1945 General Election), US President Harry Truman and Stalin met at the Cecilienhof palace outside Berlin. In addition to the main agreement, on 26 July Churchill, Truman and Chiang Kai-Shek of China issued the Potsdam Declaration, demanding the surrender of Japan.

During the conference, Truman mentioned to Stalin that the US had a 'powerful new weapon', referring to the atomic bomb (which Stalin already knew of thanks to the work of Soviet intelligence); an atomic bomb had been tested at Alamogordo, New Mexico, on 16 July, the day before the Potsdam Conference started, proving that the weapon worked. On 6 August, Colonel Paul Tibbets, commander of the special USAAF unit formed to use the atomic bombs in combat, dropped the first atomic bomb, Little Boy, on Hiroshima from *Enola Gay*. Almost everything in the city within 1 mile of the point directly below the explosion was completely destroyed, except some earthquake-proof buildings whose concrete shells remained intact. The fireball from the explosion was 1,200 feet in diameter and set off a firestorm that destroyed an area of 2 miles in diameter. On 9 August *Bockscar*, piloted by Major Charles Sweeney, dropped the second atomic bomb, Fat Man, on Nagasaki. The bomb missed its planned point of detonation by almost 2 miles, resulting in less extensive damage than at Hiroshima but it is estimated that between 35,000 and 40,000 people were killed outright. Thousands more died later in both cities as a result of radiation poisoning.

The justification given for the dropping of the atomic bombs, an act unprecedented in warfare and one which has not been repeated since, was that they would force the Japanese government and armed forces to surrender without the need for an Allied invasion of the Japanese Home Islands; having seen the often suicidal resistance mounted by the Japanese defenders on Iwo Jima and Okinawa, planners had every reason to foresee heavy Allied casualties if there was an invasion of Japan itself. It has also been argued, however, that Truman wanted to avoid Soviet involvement in the terms of the Japanese surrender. Stalin had agreed that the Soviet Union would enter the war against Japan, breaking a neutrality pact signed in April 1941, and invade Japanese-occupied Manchuria (the area of northern China which Japan had invaded in 1931, sparking a bitterness between the two countries that lasts to this day) from Siberia – Soviet troops entered China and Korea on 9 August.

Reacting to the dropping of the atomic bombs and to the Soviet declaration of war, on 10 August Emperor Hirohito agreed with the opinion of his prime minister and foreign minister and the Japanese envoy to Sweden and Switzerland was instructed to inform the Allies that Japan would surrender. Despite an attempted coup by right-wingers and members of the military on the night of 14/15 August aimed at preventing it, on 15 August Emperor Hirohito addressed his people over the radio and announced that Japan would surrender and the Allies celebrated VJ Day. Famously, the poor quality of the recording and the formal classical, courtly Japanese used by the emperor meant many of his listeners were unclear as to whether Japan was surrendering or not and a radio announcer had to confirm this afterwards. The following day, 16 August, Emperor Hirohito issued an order commanding all Japanese forces to cease fire. On 22 August, Japanese forces in Manchuria surrendered to the Soviets; on 27 August the remaining Japanese forces in Burma ceremonially surrendered at Rangoon. On 30 August, a Royal Navy force arrived at Hong Kong to take the surrender of the Japanese forces there, which was officially signed on 16 September; on 31 August and 1 September, aircraft from HMS *Indomitable*, which had accompanied the Royal Navy force, flew missions against Japanese suicide boats that were attacking the British ships.

On 2 September 1945, the Japanese foreign minister Mamoru Shigemitsu signed the instrument of surrender for the Japanese armed forces on board the battleship USS *Missouri*, anchored in Tokyo Bay. General Douglas MacArthur signed as Allied Commander-in-Chief, while Admiral Chester Nimitz signed for the United States and Admiral Sir Bruce Fraser signed for Britain. The Second World War was finally officially over.

January

Ground crew watch as a B-29 Superfortress lifts off from one of the air bases on the island of Saipan, bound for Japan. The B-29s had been flying from bases in the Mariana Islands since late 1944, flying precision bombing raids, but at the start of January 1945 they switched to area bombing, attacking Nagoya on 3 January.

Smoke rising from an oil refinery at Pagkalan Brandan, on the Indonesian island of Sumatra, after it had been bombed by Grumman Avengers and Fairey Fireflies flying from aircraft carriers of the British Pacific Fleet.

The remnants of Bastogne, heavily bombed and bombarded by the Germans during the fighting for the town in December 1944 and January 1945. It was garrisoned by men of the US 101st Airborne Division.

American troops fighting in the Battle of the Bulge using white sheets to camouflage their vehicle.

Examining supplies dropped by parachute to the American troops fighting in Bastogne.

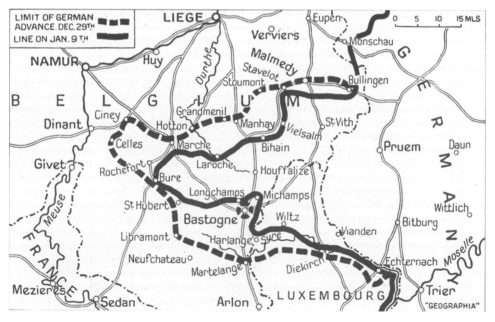

The front lines in the Battle of the Bulge as of 9 January.

Ground crew on a snowy airfield in the Low Countries using collapsible tubes to pump hot air from a van into the air intake and radiator of a Hawker Typhoon fighter bomber.

Another photograph from the winter of 1944/45. Ground crew are seen sweeping snow away from rows of 500-lb bombs ready for loading onto B-25 Mitchell medium bombers.

Two photographs showing British paratroopers in action in Athens, fighting guerrillas from ELAS.

On 9 January, American forces landed on the island of Luzon in the Philippines. In an attempt to stop the landings, the Japanese launched kamikaze attacks on the invasion forces; in this photograph, a Japanese bomber has crashed into the sea just ahead of a US Navy battleship.

The crew of a 20-mm anti-aircraft gun aboard a landing craft off the coast of the Philippines prepare to fire at attacking Japanese aircraft.

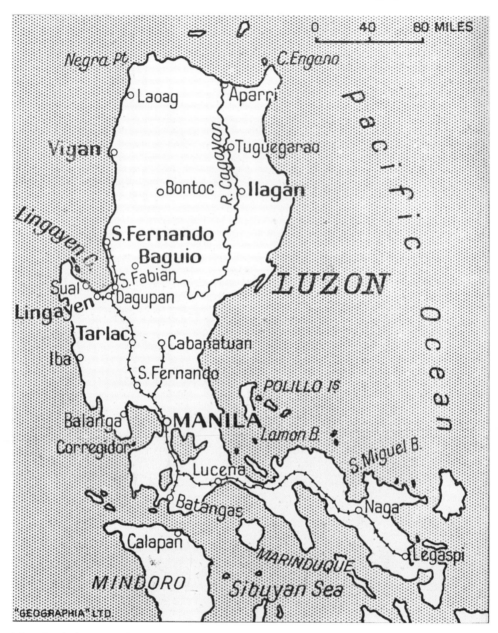

The island of Luzon. The American troops landed in the Lingayen Gulf on the west coast of the island.

An RAF Dakota transport drops supplies to East African troops fighting on the east bank of Burma's Chindwin River with a Bofors gun crew in the foreground to protect the aircraft.

HMS *Indomitable*, one of the six fleet carriers in the British Pacific Fleet.

Grumman Avenger bombers on the flight deck of one of the British Pacific Fleet aircraft carriers. At the end of January, Royal Navy aircraft launched two attacks against Japanese-held oil refineries on the Indonesian island of Sumatra. In total, forty-eight of the aircraft involved were lost.

The flight crew of 'D for Dorothy', an RAF Mosquito of the Meteorological Flight on stand-by to take off for a weather reconnaissance mission.

'D for Dorothy' in flight. This Mosquito was one of two attached to the Meteorological Flight; for three years the two aircraft flew over Germany prior to every major RAF and USAAF bombing raid, collecting weather data.

A very grainy photograph of what appears to be an Ilyushin Il-2 Shturmovik, one of the most widely produced and important Soviet aircraft of the Second World War, flying over the ruins of Budapest. The battle for the city lasted from 26 December 1944 into February 1945.

Another famous central European capital captured by Soviet forces. The ruins of Warsaw were captured by forces that included men of the Polish First Army, on 17 January 1945. The city had been badly damaged by German bombing and artillery bombardment during the uprising by the Polish Home Army in the second half of 1944.

Warsaw's Market Square following the liberation of the city from the Germans by Soviet forces.

An artist's impression of an Allied air attack on a concentrated column of German armoured vehicles, lorries and guns retreating back towards Germany through the Siegfried Line following the Battle of the Bulge.

On 20 January, a unit of Gloster Meteor F.3s, the RAF's first operational jet fighter, was deployed to an airfield in Belgium, having been judged ready for combat over Europe. Meteors had seen action for the first time in the summer of 1944, shooting down V-1 flying bombs over southern England. Although the Meteor pilots hoped they would get the chance to fly against the Messerschmitt Me 262, they were forbidden from flying east of Eindhoven or over German-occupied territory to prevent the Germans (or the Soviets) from capturing an example.

A Bristol Beaufighter of the RAF's Balkan Air Force on patrol, four of its eight rockets visible under the starboard wing.

Ground crew from the 2nd Tactical Air Force rolling a 1,000-lb bomb along the ground at an airfield in the Netherlands with a Hawker Typhoon in the background.

February

A B-17 of the Eighth Air Force over Berlin on 3 February, when 1,000 heavy bombers dropped some 2,500 tons of bombs on the city in less than an hour. The vapour trail from the bomber is mingling with the clouds of smoke from fires on the ground.

A Grumman TBF Avenger bomber flying over the mountains of Luzon, the largest island of the Philippines. At the start of February, US forces began the battle to liberate Manila; General MacArthur, the American Commander, who had also led the US forces that resisted the Japanese invasion of the Philippines, tried to restrict US air and artillery support in an attempt to prevent too much destruction in the city.

Heinsberg, in western Germany, after an attack by RAF aircraft flying close air support missions for Allied troops on the ground.

Between 4 and 11 February 1945, Churchill, Roosevelt and Stalin met at the Livadia Palace near the Crimean Black Sea resort of Yalta. They discussed the post-war shape of Europe and Stalin agreed to enter the war against Japan. In this photograph, Stalin and Roosevelt seem to be commenting on Churchill's fur hat.

One of the sessions of the Yalta Conference. Roosevelt can be seen in the centre of the photograph, Stalin to the left and Churchill to the right.

The German city of Kleve, once capital of the Duchy of Cleves (famous as the home of Anne of Cleves), was bombed particularly heavily on the night of 7/8 February, just before it was occupied by Allied forces. Over 90 per cent of the city's buildings were destroyed during the war.

Another image from the former Duchy of Cleves. This photograph shows the ruins of the town of Uedem, which like Kleve was heavily damaged by several bombing raids, as well as by the fighting that led to its capture by British and Canadian troops.

An artist's impression of the first night of the bombing of Dresden, 13/14 February. Between 13 and 15 February, raids by the USAAF and RAF devastated more than 6.5 km² of the city centre, with as many as 25,000 people thought to have been killed. Although it has been argued that Dresden was a legitimate target, a military and industrial centre and an important part of the German defences against the advancing Red Army, and that its bombing might help hasten the end of the war, critics have pointed out that the city was a cultural landmark and that the destruction was not proportionate with the military gains.

Ground crew at the base of a Royal Canadian Air Force bomber squadron wheel a 4,000-lb bomb towards the bomb bay of one of the squadron's Handley Page Halifax bombers. 500 tons of high explosives were dropped on Dresden on the night of 13/14 February.

A map showing the position of Dresden relative to the front line of the advancing troops of Marshal Ivan Koniev's First Ukrainian Front at the end of January.

RAF Liberators turn for home after bombing a Japanese supply and communications centre at Armapura, near the Burmese city of Mandalay, with smoke rising from their target. In mid-February, the Indian 19th Division launched an attack towards the city from bridgeheads on the east bank of the Irrawaddy River.

Sunderland flying boats of the RAF undergoing maintenance at a base on the island of Sri Lanka. Patrols by Sunderland and Catalina flying boats over convoys of Allied shipping in the Pacific and Indian oceans helped keep away Japanese submarines and warships.

Opposite: B-17 Flying Fortresses and their crew back at base after a raid on positions behind the German lines in support of troops from the US Ninth Army as they attempted to cross the River Roer on their way towards the Rhine.

Smoke rises near the town of Marienau after Republic P-47 Thunderbolts made a dive-bombing attack in support of troops of the US Seventh Army.

A 40-mm Bofors gun in a position on the edge of an airfield in France opens fire at a Luftwaffe raider. Although the Luftwaffe's activity had been limited, by lack of fuel in particular, it could still make its presence felt.

A slightly bad quality photograph showing the US 4th Marine Division landing on the beaches of Iwo Jima on 19 February. The island of Iwo Jima, part of Japan itself, was about 700 miles south-east of Tokyo.

The Iwo Jima landings were heavily supported by the US Navy, including escort carriers to provide close air support for the Marines. This photograph shows two aircraft carriers of the US Pacific Fleet, followed by battleships and cruisers.

Training paratroopers on the ground (above) and in an aircraft (below). Although some of the biggest airborne operations of the war in Europe, D-Day and Arnhem, were over, the losses from those battles needed to be made good as no-one knew whether more airborne assaults might be needed. The crossing of the Rhine, for example, was still to come.

Using a line of bombs as stepping stones, this airman is trying to keep his feet dry on a flooded airfield in Italy.

March

A South African Air
Force Beaufighter
fires rockets at
a target in the
Yugoslavian town
of Zuzemperk, in
the Dinaric Alps
in what is now
Slovenia. In the
foreground, smoke
can be seen drifting
towards the town's
castle, dating from
around 1000.

Supplies being dropped by parachute from an American-made C-47 Dakota of the RAF to troops of General Slim's 14th Army beyond the Irrawaddy River and advancing through Burma.

American troops in the streets of Cologne with the towers of the cathedral in the background, showing some of the devastation inflicted by the bombing campaign.

On 14 March, the railway viaduct at Bielefeld was attacked again by 617 Squadron and finally put out of service by using, for the first time, 22,000-lb Grand Slam earthquake bombs designed by Barnes Wallis.

Opposite above: The Ludendorff bridge over the Rhine at Remagen, taken by American troops on 7 March, was the first bridge across the river to be captured by Allied forces and one of only two left standing by the time of its capture.

Opposite below: The bridge was so important that the Germans launched massive air attacks in an attempt to destroy it. These included attacks by Arado Ar 234 and Messerschmitt Me 262 jets and eleven V2 rockets. This photograph shows some of the American anti-aircraft defences around the bridge.

A Grand Slam bomb being moved away on a pulley after being filled with high explosives. The men around the bomb give an idea of its size.

On 19 March, the aircraft carrier USS *Franklin* was within 50 miles of the Japanese mainland, conducting a fighter sweep over the island of Honshu and attacks on shipping in Kobe harbour. She was attacked by a single aircraft from low level, which dropped two 250-kg armour-piercing bombs.

Some of the crew of the *Franklin* waiting to be rescued from the stricken aircraft carrier are seen circled in this photograph. The two Japanese bombs caused a fuel explosion on the *Franklin*'s hangar deck and more explosions among aircraft being refuelled and rearmed on the flight deck.

The aircraft carriers HMS *Victorious* and HMS *Illustrious*, part of the British Pacific Fleet. In March 1945 the British Pacific Fleet became Task Force 57, part of the US Navy's Fifth Fleet, prior to fighting in the invasion of the island of Okinawa.

HMS *Implacable*, another of the aircraft carriers in the British Pacific Fleet.

Norway was still occupied by a significant force of German troops and aircraft. This photograph, taken from the flight deck of an escort carrier, shows the smoke from a torpedo-carrying Junkers Ju 88 which had been shot down while attacking a convoy carrying supplies around the northern tip of Norway to the USSR.

A ship under attack by de Havilland Mosquitoes of RAF Coastal Command in the harbour at Ålesund in occupied Norway on 17 March.

Another attack on shipping in Norwegian coastal waters by Coastal Command Mosquitoes, this time a raid on shipping in Dalsfjord on 23 March, led by a Norwegian pilot.

Preparing an RAF Hurricane for an armed reconnaissance mission in Burma.

On 20 March, the city of Mandalay fell to the Allied forces advancing through Burma. These two photographs show some of the air support for the ground troops. The upper image shows Sir Keith Park, commander of the Allied air forces in South East Asia and former commander of Fighter Command's 11 Group during the Battle of Britain, talking to ground crew on Ramree Island off the south coast of Burma. The lower image shows two RAF Thunderbolt fighters on an airfield near Arakan, with a B-29 bomber in the background.

One of the landing zones for Allied airborne troops on the east bank of the Rhine. A crashed glider can be seen in the foreground while Allied troops can be seen taking away one of the first prisoners to be captured.

Opposite above: A series of Hamilcar gliders and Short Stirling bombers being used as towing aircraft on an airfield before the airborne attack that was a key part of the Allied crossing of the River Rhine, Operation Plunder, on 23 March.

Opposite below: The armada in the air: gliders and aircraft flying over a bend in the Rhine.

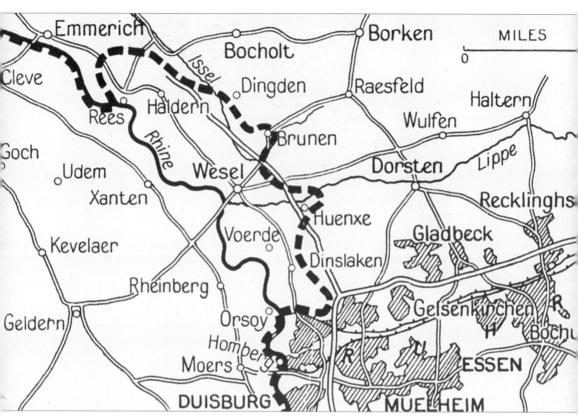

The bridgehead made on the east bank of the Rhine by Field Marshal Montgomery's 21st Army Group of British and Canadian troops.

A parachute drop of supplies to the airborne troops on the east bank of the Rhine from transport aircraft flying as low as 200 feet.

Two Royal Navy escort carriers of the British Pacific Fleet in rough seas in the Pacific with aircraft parked on their flight decks.

April

The invasion of Okinawa. It was hoped that this island, within 400 miles of the Home Islands of Japan, would provide valuable air bases for mounting further attacks. The invasion provoked fierce fighting, including the intensive use of kamikaze attacks against the supporting warships.

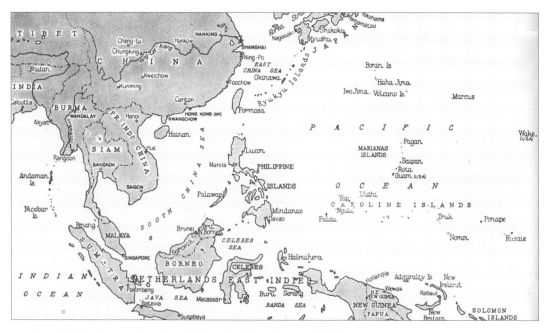

The Pacific theatre, showing the islands of Iwo Jima and Okinawa.

The British Pacific Fleet and its carriers joined the American force in support of the invasion of Okinawa, attacking airfields in the Sakishima islands, south of Okinawa, which might be used to launch kamikaze attacks. This photograph shows Vought Corsair fighters and Fairey Barracuda bombers on the flight deck of HMS *Illustrious*.

On 6 April, while screening minesweepers off the island of Ie Shima as part of the Okinawa task force, the destroyer USS *Newcomb* was hit by five kamikaze attacks over a period of an hour and a half. The upper picture shows *Newcomb* at anchor while on her way to a shipyard for repairs. The lower picture shows more clearly the damage caused during the attacks.

After the crossing of the Rhine, many of the paratroopers fought as infantry as the Allied forces advanced. This photograph shows American paratroopers on a British Churchill tank in a village on the road to the city of Münster.

British paratroopers also fought as infantry during the advance through Germany. Here, men of the 6th Airborne are seen passing through the town of Brelingen, the streets lined with Frenchmen, either prisoners of war from 1940 or men who were later forced to come to Germany to work.

The extent of the advance by Allied troops into Germany and the Netherlands as of 17 April.

Above: An aerial view of the Krupp Works at Essen in the Ruhr. One of the most famous German industrial centres, the Krupp plant stretched for 2½ miles.

Opposite above: As the advance by the forces on the ground continued, Allied air power was used to make sure that the supply lines could keep up with the front line. This photograph shows Dakota transport aircraft of the RAF on an airfield in Belgium; having brought up supplies, they would fly back with wounded men and those going home on leave.

Opposite below: Another way of using air power to maintain lines of communication. In this photograph, RAF ground crew are unloading an L5 Sentinel light aircraft from a landing craft to a beach in Burma. The L5 was used extensively in Burma to transport casualties from the front line back to clearing stations.

This photograph, taken in Hanover after its capture on 11 April, shows the destruction caused by bombing around a railway yard and large factory in the city centre.

The River Rhine and the bridge that connected Homberg and Duisberg, a major inland port for the Ruhr industrial area and one of the most heavily bombed cities in Germany during the Second World War. The city was captured by American troops on 12 April.

Two close-up views of an Me 262 jet fighter. This example was captured intact by troops of the US Seventh Army at an airfield at Giebelstadt. Coming into service before the British Gloster Meteor, the Me 262 was the world's first operational jet fighter.

A trainload of V-2 rockets thought to have been en route to a launch site, captured by troops of the US First Army at Bromskirchen.

The island of Heligoland was an important German naval base in the North Sea, just off the country's north-western coast. On 18 April, more than 900 Allied aircraft attacked Heligoland; these two photographs show the island in November 1944 and after the raid, following which the island was evacuated. In a follow-up raid on 19 April, Lancasters from 9 Squadron and 617 Squadron attacked coastal batteries on Heligoland with 12,000-lb Tallboy bombs.

On 25 April, Hitler's holiday home, the Berghof, near Berchtesgaden in the Bavarian Alps, was attacked by RAF Bomber Command, including by aircraft of 617 Squadron carrying 12,000-lb Tallboy bombs. The photograph above shows Hitler's compound at Berchtesgaden, with the SS barracks centre left, partly covered by smoke, and the Berghof itself centre bottom. The photograph below shows some of the pilots who flew the escorting Mustang fighters being debriefed on their return.

A new mission for Bomber Command's Lancaster pilots as the war came to an end. In late April, with the agreement of the occupying German forces following negotiations that came after an appeal from Prince Bernhard, the son-in-law of Queen Wilhelmina of the Netherlands, the RAF began dropping food to Dutch civilians in Operation Manna.

These two images, dated 29 April, show four-engined heavy bombers flying low and in daylight over what appears to be the Netherlands, presumably on a mission for Operations Manna and Chowhound. (J&C McCutcheon Collection)

Officers from the US First Army examining some of the 55,000 gas bombs found in a depot outside the town of Lassa.

May

On 1 May, a force of British and Gurkha paratroopers landed at Elephant Island, down river from the Burmese city of Rangoon (now Yangon). This was the beginning of the liberation of the city from the Japanese.

A closer photograph showing the Gurkha paratroopers checking their parachute harnesses before setting off for Rangoon.

The invasion force steams up the Rangoon River on 2 May, with smoke rising from the banks of the river after air strikes in support of the attack.

A Grumman Avenger torpedo bomber of the Royal Navy flies over the aircraft carrier HMS *Indomitable* as it returns from a mission attacking airfields in the Sakishima Islands in support of the fighting on Okinawa.

Bombs dropped by Royal Navy Grumman Avengers bursting on the runway of one of the airfields in the Sakishima Islands, attacked to prevent their being used as bases for kamikaze missions, in May 1945.

The unconditional surrender of German forces in Italy and Austria was announced on 2 May, although the actual surrender came on 29 April. This photograph shows the signing of the surrender document at Caserta in Campania, Southern Italy – the headquarters of the Supreme Allied Commander in Italy. The two German delegates are on the left and the Allied representatives on the right.

The remains of Rangoon railway station, heavily bombed by the Allied air forces as part of the disruption of Japanese supply and communication lines.

Supermarine Seafire and Grumman Wildcat fighters on the deck of the aircraft carrier HMS *Formidable*. On 4 May, *Formidable* was attacked and damaged by a kamikaze pilot in a Mitsubishi Zero fighter.

The ceasefire and surrender of German forces in north-west Germany, Denmark and the Netherlands came on 4 May. Here, Field Marshal Bernard Montgomery is seen reading over the surrender terms at his headquarters on Lüneberg Heath in Lower Saxony while the German envoys look on.

The German peace envoys walking away from Montgomery's headquarters after signing the surrender document. The envoys included General Admiral von Friedeburg (chief of the German navy, the Kriegsmarine), Rear-Admiral Wagner and General Kienzel.

On 5 May, Hermann Göring, who had been placed under arrest on suspicion of seeking to overthrow Hitler, was released by Luftwaffe troops. On 6 May, he surrendered to American troops in Radstadt, near Salzburg in Austria.

On 7 May, German delegates met representatives of Britain, the USSR and the US at General Eisenhower's Supreme Headquarters at Rheims. This photograph shows the delegates meeting; the German representatives have their backs to the camera, while the Allied representatives face it.

General Eisenhower making a speech during the meeting with the German delegates with his deputy, the RAF's Air Chief Marshal Tedder, sitting beside him.

8 May, VE Day, saw the terms agreed at Rheims the previous day ratified at the Soviet headquarters in Berlin. In this photograph, the Soviet deputy commander-in-chief Marshal Georgi Zhukov is signing the surrender agreement.

Field Marshal Keitel signing for the German army. The chief of the Oberkommando der Wehrmacht, or Supreme Command of the German Armed Forces, Keitel would stand trial at Nuremberg in 1946. Found guilty on all charges, Keitel was hanged.

Colonel-General Hans-Jürgen Stumpf signing the surrender for the Luftwaffe. Stumpf, who had commanded Luftflotte 5 in Norway during the Battle of Britain, launching attacks against Scotland and the north of England, was released from prison in 1947 and survived until 1968.

The king and queen, princesses Elizabeth and Margaret and Winston Churchill on the balcony at Buckingham Palace as the crowds cheer on VE Day, 8 May.

Winston Churchill is mobbed by crowds as he makes his way to the House of Commons after broadcasting the announcement of Germany's unconditional surrender from 10 Downing Street.

On 11 May, this party of British paratroopers was landed by a Short Stirling at Gardemoen Airport, Oslo, as part of the Allied force sent to Norway following the surrender of the German forces there.

On 11 May, the aircraft carrier USS *Bunker Hill* was hit twice by kamikaze pilots, each of whom dropped a 500-lb bomb on the ship before crashing onto the flight deck. The picture above shows water streaming off the deck of the carrier as the crew attempted to fight the fires, while the picture below shows the hole left in the wooden flight deck by one of the bombs.

An artist's impression of one of the convoys of surrendered U-boats moving towards internment at Londonderry, escorted by warships and Coastal Command aircraft. The convoys began on 14 May and each was escorted by a Short Sunderland flying boat, a Vickers Wellington equipped with a Leigh searchlight and a Liberator.

A photograph taken on 22 May showing a railway bridge across the straits between Singapore and the Malay Peninsula collapsing amid exploding bombs from an RAF Liberator.

Another image taken from a Liberator showing a train burning after coming under attack from the air. According to the original caption for the photograph, the train was thought to have been transporting fuel oil for the Japanese forces.

A B-25 Mitchell bomber is caught flying over a Japanese warship with its bomb bay doors open in this photograph. According to the original caption, the warship sank 'a few seconds' after the photograph was taken.

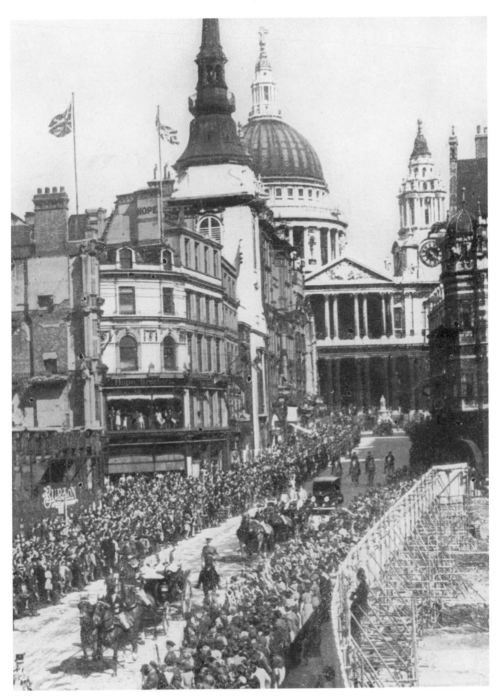

On 13 May, the first Sunday following VE Day, there was a Thanksgiving service led by the king and queen at St Paul's Cathedral. This photograph shows the royal procession passing down Ludgate Hill after the service.

June

'Z for Zebra', a Short
Sunderland V flying
boat, carried out
Coastal Command's
last convoy escort
patrol for the Royal
Navy. Patrolling 500
miles south-west of
Ireland, the crew
received the order
'Cease patrol' at one
minute past midnight
on 4 June.

The king and queen and princesses Elizabeth and Margaret are seen on a tour of south London, driving through Deptford. Damage from bombing raids and attacks by V-1 Flying Bombs and V-2 rockets can clearly be seen.

Liberated prisoners of war, having disembarked from an RAF Lancaster, wait to be driven away from the flight line in a lorry. Returning former prisoners of war was one of the RAF's big jobs after the end of the fighting in Europe.

The ruins of the German naval base at Kiel on the Baltic coast, showing the effects of the heavy bombing raids that had been carried out against the city between late February and late April 1945. In the foreground the bows of two U-boats can be seen, while in the background the wreck of the pocket battleship *Admiral Scheer* can be seen. The *Admiral Scheer* had been hit by RAF bombers in a raid on 9 April.

Pre-fabricated sections of submarine hulls in a dockyard in Bremen, which was heavily bombed by RAF Bomber Command in order to disrupt the production of U-boats.

An artist's impression of one of the raids by incendiary-carrying B-29 Superfortress bombers against Japanese cities. In this image, the target is Tokyo and the bombers can be briefly seen among the clouds of smoke from the ground, flying through searchlight beams.

B-29s on their way to the Japanese Home Islands.

Fires rage as more incendiary bombs can be seen falling to the right of the photograph.

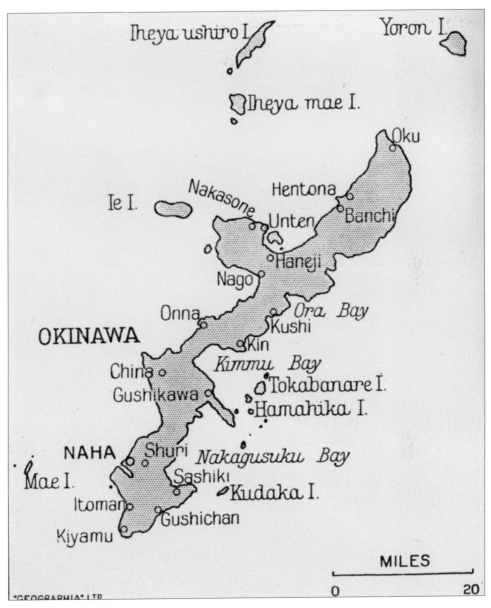

On 17 May, the capital of Okinawa, Naha, had fallen to the US forces that had been fighting on the island since the start of April.

A US Marine Corps artillery spotter plane flying on a mission over Okinawa, with smoke rising from where artillery and mortars had been firing on Japanese strongpoints.

A Japanese aircraft, hit by anti-aircraft guns and on fire, passes over an escort carrier of the US Navy off the coast of Okinawa.

A kamikaze aircraft plunges into the water just short of its target, a battleship in the US Navy task force off Okinawa, after being hit by anti-aircraft fire from several nearby warships.

The Yokosuka MXY7 Ohka (Cherry blossom) was a rocket-powered, human-guided anti-shipping weapon designed specifically to be used by kamikaze pilots. The Americans nicknamed the Ohka 'Baka' (Japanese for 'idiot'). This example, captured during the fighting on Okinawa, is seen being examined by a group of US Marines.

Japanese aircraft crash into the sea among the Allied fleet during a heavy attack off Okinawa.

1. In a steel mill at Republic Steel in Ohio, molten iron is being blown in a Bessemer converter to transform it into steel to make weapons and munitions. (LoC)

2. Assembling part of the cowling for a bomber engine at the North American Aviation plant in Inglewood, California. (LoC)

3. A P-51 Mustang fighter under construction at another North American Aviation plant in California, this time in Los Angeles. (LoC)

4. Two female workers at North American Aviation assembling a section of a wing for a P-51 Mustang. (LoC)

5. Mechanics working on the engine of a C-47 transport plane at the Douglas Aircraft Company plant in Long Beach, California. (LoC)

6. Female workers inspecting parts for the wings of C-47 transport planes at the Douglas Aircraft Company plant at Long Beach. (LoC)

Above and below: 7. and 8. Two images of women workers using a hand drill to assemble panels for dive bombers at the Vultee plant in Nashville, Tennessee. (LoC)

9. Working on the tail of a US Navy aircraft in the assembly and repair department of Corpus Christi Naval Air Station, Texas. (LoC)

Above and below: 10. and 11. Two images showing Marine glider pilots being trained at Page Field on Parris Island, South Carolina. (LoC)

12. A pilot climbs into the cockpit of an aircraft at Corpus Christi Naval Air Station. (LoC)

13. A cadet pilot examines the propeller of a training biplane. (LoC)

14. A close-up of a Consolidated PBY Catalina flying boat drawn up on the ramp at Corpus Christi Naval Air Station. (LoC)

15. Pulling a Catalina flying boat out of the water and up a ramp at Corpus Christi Naval Air Station. (LoC)

16. Carrying out maintenance on the engines of a Catalina flying boat. The Catalina was powered by two Pratt & Whitney Twin Wasp 1,200 hp radial engines. (LoC)

17. A B-17 Flying Fortress silhouetted on its airfield by the setting sun. (LoC)

18. The crew of a B-17 receive their final instructions in the shadow of their aircraft just prior to climbing on board. (LoC)

19. A B-17 pilot photographed just before climbing into the cockpit of his aircraft prior to take-off. (LoC)

20. Three B-17 Flying Fortresses are seen with a P-51 Mustang escort fighter, *The Iowa Beaut* of the 355th Fighter Group. (USAF)

21. A crew walk away from their B-24 Liberator bomber after a mission over Europe. (USAF)

22. USAAF ground crew are sitting beside a spotter plane parked in front of a Flying Fortress. These photographs show something of the size of a four-engined heavy bomber. (USAF)

23. A priest offers his blessing to the crew of a B-17 Flying Fortress before they take off for a mission over Germany. (USAF)

24. A US poster appealing for funds for the seventh war loan in 1945, using imagery taken from the famous photograph of US Marines raising the US flag over Mount Suribachi on Iwo Jima. (LoC)

25. A US propaganda poster preparing the American public for the task of invading Japan after the end of the war in Europe. It was partly to avoid the massive US casualties that it was predicted would result from an invasion of Japan itself that the atomic bombs were dropped on Hiroshima and Nagasaki. (NARA)

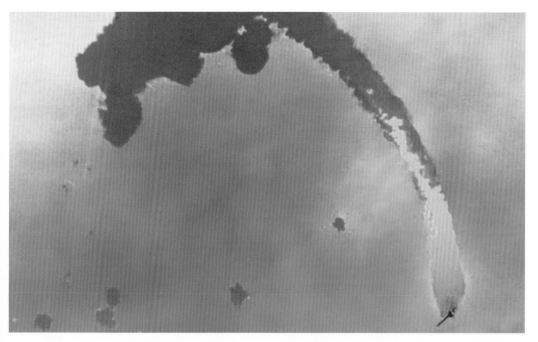

26. A somewhat lurid colour image of a Japanese Mitsubishi G4M Betty bomber that had been shot down in flames over the Ryukyu islands, the island group that includes Okinawa and the Sakishima islands. (J&C McCutcheon Collection)

27. A US Navy sailor and his girlfriend in front of the Tomb of the Unknown Soldier in Arlington National Cemetery, Virginia. An unknown American soldier from the Second World War, along with one from the Korean War, was buried alongside his comrade from the First World War. (LoC)

28. Dr Werner von Braun, photographed behind his desk as the director of the Marshall Space Flight Centre in 1964, where he worked on the Saturn V rocket that would propel Neil Armstrong, Buzz Aldrin and Michael Collins to the Moon in 1969. (NASA)

Above: Smoke pouring from an aircraft carrier hit by a kamikaze pilot off Okinawa.

Below: Fire-fighters in action after a kamikaze pilot had crashed into the flight deck of a British aircraft carrier. Thanks to their steel flight decks (as opposed to the wooden flight decks on US aircraft carriers), British aircraft carriers were not as vulnerable to kamikaze attacks but they could still cause heavy damage.

Inspecting damage to the bridge of HMS *Illustrious* after a kamikaze attack while the carrier was serving as part of the British task force attacking the Sakashima islands. The damage was only relatively slight, because the Japanese aircraft scraped the bridge with its wing before crashing into the sea.

The US Navy at anchor in Ulithi Atoll in the Gilbert Islands. Six Essex-class aircraft carriers can be seen here, as can an Independence-class aircraft carrier, to the left of the photograph.

Loading a Grumman F6F Hellcat fighter with air-to-ground rockets on board an escort carrier of the British Pacific Fleet.

A Fairey Firefly, also loaded with air-to-ground rockets, sitting on the flight deck of one of the British Pacific Fleet's fleet aircraft carriers.

A collapsed bridge on the Bangkok–Singapore Railway around 600 miles to the north of Singapore, with a bomb exploding near the river bank. The photograph was taken from one of the RAF Liberators that flew a round trip of nearly 2,500 miles from bases in India to attack the bridge.

July

A depot near Munich, in the American zone of occupation in Germany, crowded with B-17 Flying Fortresses parked wingtip to wingtip. Some of these bombers, no longer needed in Europe, might have been intended to make their way out to the Pacific.

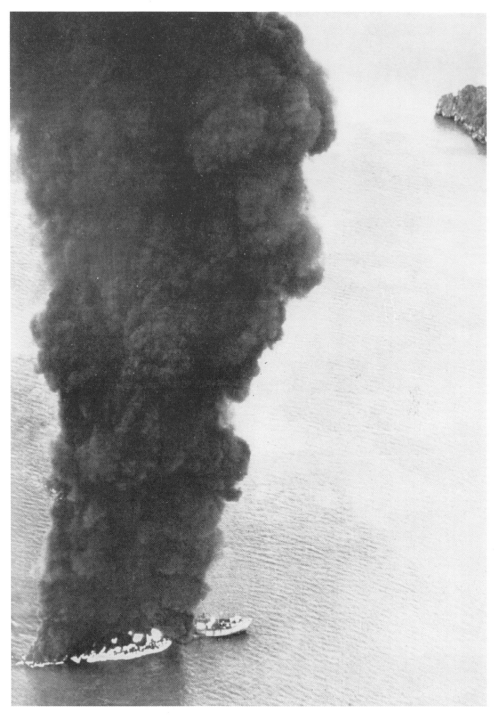

A thick plume of black smoke rising from a Japanese tanker after an Allied air attack which, according to the original caption, had taken place some time before the photograph was taken from a Liberator bomber.

One of the airfields on Guam from which the B-29 Superfortresses flew their raids against Japanese cities. This photograph, as with that on page 102, gives an idea of the scale of the US war effort by this time.

A Consolidated PBY Catalina flying boat returning from a patrol to its base on what was then Ceylon, now Sri Lanka, in an idyllic photograph.

RAF armourers lifting depth charges out of a boat and onto the wing of a Catalina flying boat at one of the bases on Sri Lanka. Although the strength of the Japanese navy had been greatly reduced, there was still a threat to Allied convoys from Japanese submarines.

Airlifting stores to the troops in the front line was also key to keeping the Allied forces in Burma adequately supplied. In this photograph, an auxiliary fuel tank is being loaded on board a Dakota of RAF Transport Command.

A bridge over the Meklong river at Kanchanaburi, west of Bangkok, bombed by RAF Liberators to disrupt communications between the Japanese forces in Burma and those in what was then Siam, now Thailand.

J. Robert Oppenheimer, Professor of Physics at University of California, Berkeley, and head of the research laboratory at the Manhattan Project. On 16 July, the Manhattan Project detonated an atomic bomb in the Trinity Test in New Mexico. (NARA)

Italian physicist Enrico Fermi, who led the team that demonstrated the first artificial, self-sustaining nuclear chain reaction. A member of the Manhattan Project team, Fermi headed the team working on thermonuclear weapons. (NARA)

Above and overleaf: Some of the cutting-edge scientific equipment needed in the development of the atomic bomb: a particle accelerator at the University of Notre Dame (above) and a cyclotron, another form of particle accelerator developed by Ernest O. Lawrence, who was also a member of the Manhattan Project.

The Oak Ridge facility in Tennessee where plutonium and uranium-235 for the development of nuclear weapons were separated and transmuted.

The Trinity Test explosion 16 milliseconds after detonation on 16 July. The Trinity device was the same type as that which would be detonated over Nagasaki. (NARA)

In July 1945, aircraft of the British Pacific Fleet were operating over the Sea of Japan, between the Japanese Home Islands and the mainland of Asia, and sank several Japanese warships, including an escort carrier. The above photograph shows a Fairey Barracuda preparing to take off from the flight deck of a British aircraft carrier in the Pacific, while the lower photograph shows a formation of Grumman Hellcat and Martlet fighters in formation over the flight deck of another carrier.

Two very different images of aircraft returning to the aircraft carrier HMS *Indefatigable* after air operations against the Japanese. That above shows a Supermarine Seafire that had crashed on landing on the carrier, while the image below shows the wings of a Fairey Firefly being folded away to save space before being returned to the hangar under the flight deck.

An artist's impression of an operation carried out by the British Pacific Fleet at the end of July to clear a way through minefields along the west coast of Thailand (then Siam) and the west coast of the Malay Peninsula towards the Malacca Strait and Singapore. Fighter cover from aircraft carriers with the force helped protect the ships from air attacks, including kamikaze attacks.

A blurry but graphic photograph of the Japanese battleship *Haruna* under attack from British and US carrier aircraft while at anchor at the naval base of Kure on 28 July. *Haruna* had been lightly damaged in an attack four days previously, but was attacked again and sank later on the 28th.

A Japanese car ferry bombed by carrier aircraft in the Tsugaru Straits between the islands of Hokkaido and Honshu.

August

Harry S. Truman, the thirty-third President of the United States, succeeded President Roosevelt when he died of a cerebral haemorrhage in April 1945. In August, he approved the use of the atomic bomb against Japan in the hope that it would bring about a surrender without an invasion (forecast to result in as many as half a million American casualties).

An artist's impression of the explosion of the first atomic bomb on Hiroshima on 6 August.

A map of Japan showing the locations of both Hiroshima and Nagasaki as well as other cities such as Tokyo and Nagoya that had been heavily bombed with conventional weapons.

The mushroom cloud following the explosion of the Fat Man atomic bomb on Nagasaki on 9 August. The cloud at this point was more than 20,000 feet high. An implosion weapon using plutonium, Fat Man was similar to the Trinity Test bomb.

A photograph by a Japanese photographer showing a group of survivors moving through the devastation in Nagasaki after the dropping of the atomic bomb.

Three pilots walking away from their Spitfires across a muddy airfield after a mission to provide close air support to the army along the River Sittang in eastern Burma.

Supermarine Seafires, with their good performance at high altitude and relative lack of ability to carry weapons like bombs and rockets, were used to fly combat air patrols over the ships of the British Pacific Fleet. 15 August was their most successful day, shooting down eight attacking aircraft for one loss. This photograph shows a Seafire fitted with rockets designed to help heavily-laden aircraft take off from aircraft carriers more easily.

Hauling a Catalina flying boat up a slipway prior to a maintenance check at Korangi Creek, Karachi, which was one of the main bases for maintaining the RAF Catalina and Sunderland flying boats in the Far East.

Grumman Avengers of the British Pacific Fleet flying over some British warships on their way to bomb targets on the Japanese Home Islands.

The airfield of Takamatsu on the island of Shikoku in the south of Japan, with bombs from carrier-borne Fleet Air Arm aircraft exploding on it. The British Pacific Fleet was operating as part of Admiral Halsey's US 3rd Fleet at this point.

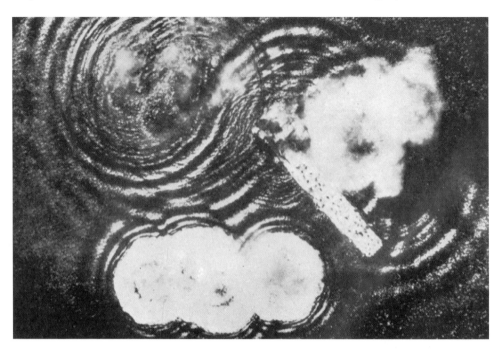

Above: Smoke and shock waves from bombs can be seen surrounding this Japanese escort carrier under attack from carrier-borne Grumman Avenger aircraft.

Below: Crewmen on board a US Navy Essex-class aircraft carrier from the 3rd Fleet loading rockets onto the wings of an aircraft about to take off for a mission attacking targets on the Japanese Home Islands.

Above and overleaf: Although the war in the Far East was coming to an end, carrier aviation was still in itself a dangerous activity, despite the reduction in Japanese military activity. In the photograph above, a bulldozer is seen clearing away a Hellcat fighter that had turned over onto its back after missing the arrester wire while landing. In the lower photograph, a Fairey Barracuda has crashed onto the fo'c'sle of the aircraft carrier after running off the flight deck while taxiing.

Fireworks soaring over the roofs of London and into the Thames on VJ Day, 15 August, as seen from Westminster Bridge.

The royal family leaving St Paul's Cathedral on Sunday 19 August after a service to give thanks for the end of the war.

The aircraft carrier HMS *Indomitable*, her deck crowded with Fairey Barracudas and Grumman Corsairs. She arrived to provide air support to the Royal Navy force under Rear-Admiral Harcourt that liberated Hong Kong on 30 August, her aircraft flying missions against Japanese suicide boats that were attacking the British forces.

General Douglas MacArthur, left, watches the Japanese foreign minister, Shigemitsu, signing the surrender document on board the battleship USS *Missouri* in Tokyo Bay on 3 September. The war was finally over.

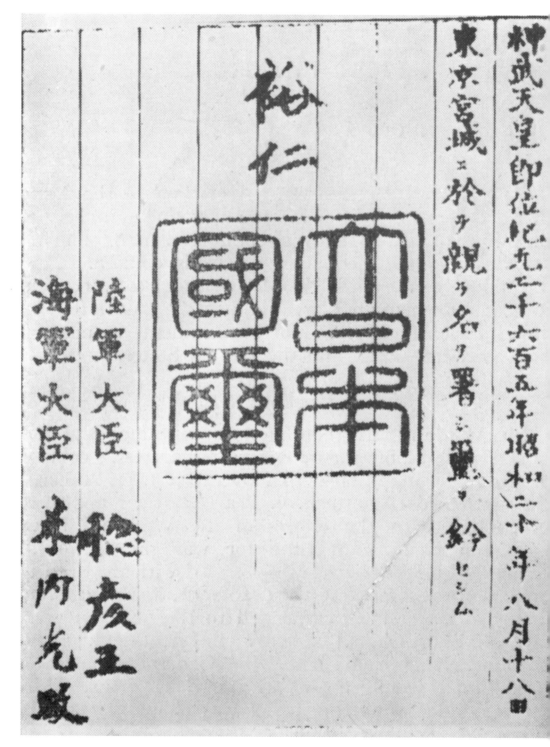

A page of the credentials presented by the Japanese delegation, showing the Japanese imperial seal in the centre, with Emperor Hirohito's personal signature above.

A bad quality photograph that nonetheless says it all: British and American former prisoners of war celebrate after having been released from a camp near Tokyo.

Aftermath

The aftermath of the Second World War is, in many ways, still being felt today. Among the first of the war's repercussions came as a result of the Potsdam Conference, which met outside Berlin between July and August 1945 with the new British Prime Minister Clement Attlee, US President Harry Truman and Joseph Stalin of the Soviet Union all in attendance. They agreed, among other things, to divide Germany and Austria into zones of occupation and to demilitarise and denazify both countries; they also shifted the borders to remove Germany's eastern provinces including Prussia, Silesia and much of Pomerania and agreed to the transfer of ethnic Germans to Germany from countries such as Czechoslovakia, seeking to remove many of the justifications that Hitler had used to seize territory immediately before the start of the war. As part of the demilitarisation process, all German aircraft factories were dismantled or destroyed.

The prosecution of Nazi war criminals had also been agreed upon at the Potsdam Conference. The first trial, held between 20 November 1945 and 1 October 1946, heard the cases of twenty-three of the most senior surviving political and military leaders from Nazi Germany. The highest ranking of these was Hermann Göring. Charged with war crimes, crimes against humanity, conspiracy and waging a war of aggression, Göring pleaded that he was 'in the sense of the indictment not guilty'. Found guilty on all counts and described as 'often, indeed almost always, the moving force, second only to his leader', Göring was sentenced to be hanged but committed suicide before the sentence could be carried out. In a later trial in spring 1947, Field Marshal Milch, also of the Luftwaffe, was also charged with war crimes and crimes against humanity. Between December 1947 and October 1948, the Luftwaffe's Field Marshal Sperrle was tried as part of a group of officers from the German high command and acquitted.

Attempts by the Western Allies to develop their zones of occupation by introducing a new currency, the Deutschmark, including to the occupation zones in Berlin, led to a Soviet blockade of West Berlin. As the roads, railways and canals were all closed, the only way into the city from the west was by air so the US, helped by Britain, organised a mass airlift through the air corridors to carry in the almost 5,000 tons of supplies needed to keep 2 million Berliners fed and provided with heat and light every day. The blockade lasted from 24 June 1948 to 12 May 1949.

In addition to some of the more far-reaching technological consequences of the war, there were many short-term problems to be dealt with. The first of these was the vast quantity of weapons, ammunition and munitions scattered across the former battlefields in both Europe and Asia. These had to be gathered together and dealt with, ammunition blown up and aircraft made unusable then cut up and disposed of, or in the case of more sophisticated models, taken back to the USSR, Britain or the US for further study (for more on which, see below). Then there were the people. Former members of the German and Japanese armed forces had to be processed and those wanted for crimes committed during the war held in custody for the trials that would later come. Allied former prisoners of war had to be processed as well and returned home, many of those from Japanese-run camps in very frail physical condition. In Germany, the Allies had discovered many civilians from occupied countries, particularly from Poland and the Soviet Union, as well as Soviet prisoners of war, who had been used as forced labour and these had to be repatriated. Those repatriated to the Soviet Union faced a grim future: they would be regarded as traitors, described as 'socially dangerous', presumably for having been exposed to life outside the Soviet Union, however unpleasant, and often deported to remote parts of the country and made to carry out hard labour. Under the Yalta Agreement, the Western Allies were obligated to return Soviet or Yugoslav civilians by force if necessary and although this happened in the French and British zones, General Eisenhower banned forced repatriation in the American zone. Finally, the vast numbers of men and women who had been called up for service in the Allied armed forces had to be demobilised and prepared for their return to civilian life to help rebuild economies that had often been exhausted by the sheer effort of fighting the war, or devastated by occupation.

Most of these were things that the Allies could each deal with independently, as they saw fit, or on which they were able to cooperate. The question of captured German technology, however, was somewhat more vexed. As the war ended, the Western Allies and the Soviet Union were becoming increasingly suspicious of each other's intentions. To start with, both sides wished to take advantage of the sophisticated technical research that had been going on in Nazi Germany and there was a race to recover not only the blueprints for and examples of German technology such as rockets, jet engines and radar systems, but also the scientists who had worked on the projects. Perhaps the most famous example is Wernher von Braun, the rocket scientist who had headed the team who developed the V2 rocket. Evacuated from the Peenemünde test centre on the Baltic coast to the Bavarian Alps, out of the path of the advancing Red Army, von Braun and his team surrendered to the US Army in early May 1945. Initially employed by the US Army to work on ballistic missiles, he would later transfer to work for NASA and was involved in the development of the Saturn V rocket that would carry Apollo XI to the Moon in 1969.

As well as taking von Braun and his team into custody, the US Army had liberated the Mittelbau-Dora concentration camp in the north of Thuringia and discovered the Mittelwerk underground facility where the camp inmates had been made to work producing both the V1 and the V2. As Thuringia was due to be part of the Soviet zone of occupation, the Americans shipped out what rocket parts they could for their own use before handing over the plant, including parts, machine tools and blueprints, to the Red Army in June 1945. The Soviets aimed to effectively relocate German technical research facilities in the USSR proper, transporting to the east equipment from places such as Mittelwerk and the Luftwaffe aviation test facility at Rechlin, along with more than ninety trainloads of German specialists and their families and belongings. The Soviet technical projects, especially the development of nuclear weaponry, also had secret intelligence available as well as German technical knowhow. In 1950, Klaus Fuchs, a German-born physicist who had worked for the Manhattan Project as well as British nuclear research projects, admitted to having spied for the Soviet Union since 1942. In 1951, Julius and Ethel Rosenberg were found guilty of also passing nuclear secrets from the Manhattan Project to the Soviets, and were executed by electric chair in 1953. However, it is difficult to say how much the information from the so-called atomic spies helped the Soviet scientists, due to the way it was used by the paranoid Lavrenti Beria, head of the NVKD, who had been placed in charge of the Soviet atomic bomb project by Stalin. Nevertheless, the first Soviet atomic bomb was tested in August 1949; US intelligence had not expected this until 1953 and British intelligence expected it would take until 1954.

In April 1946, what was to become the MiG-9 became the first Soviet jet aircraft to fly. The first examples were powered by German BMW 003 engines and later ones had Soviet-made engines reverse-engineered from the German examples. However, there were problems with the engines and although the Soviets had acquired sophisticated German engine technology, it had not been fully developed; the Soviets were able to obtain a licence to build the Rolls-Royce Nene, which they mass-produced and used to power the MiG-15. The MiG-15, with its swept wings, was able to outclass straight-winged jets like the Gloster Meteor when they met during the Korean War in the early 1950s. As a result, the USAF rushed into action the North American F-86 Sabre, which was not the first American jet fighter (this distinction belongs to the Bell P-59 Airacomet) but was the first American design to be influenced by German research, which emphasised the importance of a thin, swept wing like that used on the Soviet MiG fighters. Which of the two fighters, the F-86 or the MiG-15, was superior is a question hotly debated by those that flew them in Korea.

The Cold War was now in full swing, powered in many respects by the technology developed during and immediately after the Second World War, primarily of course rocket technology and nuclear weapons.

A flight lieutenant from RAF Transport Command with a Russian woman and her young son after they had been flown to Lüneberg for repatriation back to the Soviet Union. Many Soviet slave labourers and prisoners of war faced a grim fate when they returned.

The Allied leaders at the Potsdam Conference, held just outside Berlin in July and August 1945. From left to right: Clement Attlee (Prime Minister following the 1945 General Election, the results of which were announced on 26 July), President Harry Truman and Joseph Stalin.

The third day of the Potsdam Conference, 19 July. Stalin can be seen at the top of the photograph, Clement Attlee and Winston Churchill to the left and Truman to the right.

Two photographs of the shattered ruins of Berlin – the government buildings around the Brandenburg Gate in the upper photograph and the area between the districts of Friedrichshain and Lichtenberg in the lower – taken by a low-flying RAF Mosquito after the fall of the city to the Red Army. Although some of the damage undoubtedly came from the fighting in which the city fell, much of it would have been caused by the RAF area bombing campaign.

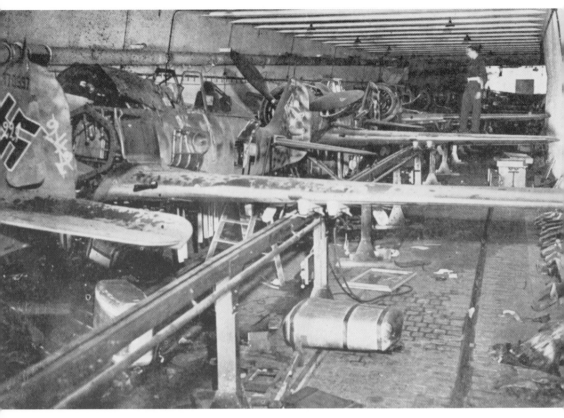

A reinforced concrete passageway underneath Berlin's Tempelhof Airport where Focke-Wulf Fw 190 fighter aircraft were assembled using parts manufactured elsewhere and brought to Berlin for assembly.

The aperture at the end of the passageway through which finished aircraft emerged ready to be test-flown.

Clearing away the debris of the bombing. The image above shows German prisoners of war clearing up rubble in Munich, while the image below shows women paid by the Russians clearing up in Berlin.

A German engineer explaining the details of a 'Bernhard' radar transmitter to RAF technical experts.

A USAAF officer poses with a German guided missile, giving an idea of the size of the weapon.

V-2 rocket engines lined up in the underground Mittelwerk factory at Nordhausen, captured by the Americans. (John Christopher Collection)

V-1 Flying Bombs lined up on an underground production line at the Mittelwerk. (John Christopher Collection)

From left to right, a US soldier, Walter Dornberger, Herbert Axter, Wernher von Braun and Hans Lindenberg after the surrender of von Braun's team to the US Army. Von Braun's name was at the top of the list of German scientists and engineers wanted for interrogation by the US military. (US Army)

Wernher von Braun (front row, seventh from the right) among a group of 104 German rocket scientists photographed at Fort Bliss, Texas, where they were working on rockets for the US Army. Many would go on to work on the Explorer 1 and Saturn space rockets. (US Army)

Chuck Yeager standing next to *Glamorous Glennis*, the Bell X-1 experimental jet in which he broke the sound barrier on 14 October 1947. (USAF)

Yeager's X-1 was carried up to the right altitude in the bomb bay of a modified B-29 and then released. This photograph shows a later X-1 being attached to a B-29 before a test flight. (NASA)

German-born physicist Klaus Fuchs fled Germany for Britain in 1933. During the Second World War, he worked on the Manhattan Project and on British nuclear projects; in 1950 he admitted spying for the Soviet Union, passing on information about nuclear technology. (National Archive)

Ethel and Julius Rosenberg, separated by a wire screen as they leave court after being found guilty of spying for the Soviet Union, passing on information from the Manhattan Project at Los Alamos among other things. They were executed by electric chair in 1953. (LoC)

A MiG 15 in USAF markings after it had been flown to South Korea by a defecting North Korean pilot. (USAF)

A two-seat training version of the North American F-86 Sabre, which fought against the MiG 15 during the Korean War. (USAF)

One of the other major problems for the Allies was to dispose of captured German and Japanese weapons, munitions and other military equipment. This photograph shows RAF personnel fitting fuses and detonators to German bombs prior to blowing them up in a controlled explosion.

A dump of German bombs disappears in a cloud of smoke.

A wing commander from the RAF's Air Disarmament Branch accepts a consignment of eighty German aircraft from a Luftwaffe technical officer in Oslo.

A line-up of Messerschmitt Me 410 aircraft with their propellers removed on an airfield near Copenhagen.

A row of abandoned Messerschmitt Me 262 jet fighters in a forest in Obertraubling, just outside the Bavarian city of Regensburg, where there was a Messerschmitt aircraft plant. (NARA)

An American pilot takes a captured Me 262 for a spin, still in its Luftwaffe markings. (NARA)

This is a Bachem Ba 349, a rocket-propelled interceptor that was designed to take off vertically, like a modern surface-to-air missile. However, the only manned vertical take-off flight made in a Ba 349 ended in the death of the test pilot. This photograph shows one of a group of Ba 349s captured by American troops in the Austrian Alps, where the Bachem team had fled after their factory was captured. (NARA)

Another unusual design: this is a Dornier Do 335 fighter-bomber, powered by a push-pull engine arrangement of engines and propellers. The Do 335 went into production in late 1944 and deliveries began in January 1945 but the pace was slow: by late April 1945, when the Dornier factory at Oberpfaffenhofen in Bavaria was captured by the US Army, only thirteen had been completed. (NARA)

The Arado Ar 234 was the world's first operational jet-powered bomber. Just over 200 were built between mid-1944 and the end of the war, perhaps the best-known example of their use being raids on the Ludendorff Bridge over the Rhine at Remagen; an Ar 234 was also the last Luftwaffe aircraft to fly over Britain. This is example is seen in RAF markings after it had been captured by British forces.

This photograph, taken in August, shows the first British General Court in Berlin.

The trial at Nuremberg of twenty-three of the most important political and military figures from Nazi Germany. This photograph of some of the defendants shows (front row, left to right) Hermann Göring, Rudolf Hess, Joachim von Ribbentrop, Wilhelm Keitel, (second row, left to right) Karl Dönitz, Erich Raeder, Baldur von Schirach and Fritz Sauckel. (US Govt)

A former member of the RAF is being fitted with his civilian suit at the Demobilisation Clothing Centre immediately before his return to civilian life at the end of the war.

Opposite: The Berlin Airlift, 1948–49. In an attempt to force the Western Allies to withdraw the new Deutschmark from use in West Berlin, the Soviets closed the road, railway and canal access from West Germany to West Berlin. The Allied response was to airlift supplies to the city. The above photograph shows a line of C-47 Skytrain transports unloading at Tempelhof Airport, while the photograph below shows a flour from the US being unloaded from a C-47 at Gatow. (USAF/NARA)

Also available from Amberley Publishing

THE SECOND WORLD WAR IN THE AIR
IN PHOTOGRAPHS

1944

L. ARCHARD

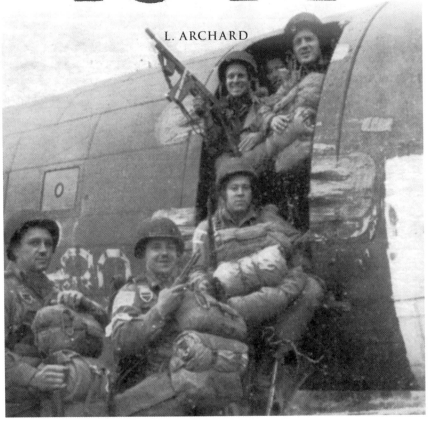

Available from all good bookshops or to order direct
Please call **01453-847-800**
www.amberleybooks.com